PRAISE FOR

BLACK STEEL MAGNOLIAS IN THE HOUR OF CHAOS THEORY

"I remember first hearing James Cagney read poems in a packed backroom in Oakland and being entirely shook by what this man can do with language. *Black Steel Magnolias in the Hour of Chaos Theory* makes good on that promise of strangeness, urgency, lyric prowess, and invention. Toggling between loss, therapy, the pastoral, illness, the humorously personable, and the darkly familial—at every turn this book surprises, aches, & delights. "what flower / cuts thru the bullshit / between people"— Do yourself a favor and read it thrice."

Sam Sax
author of *Madness*

"The poems in *Black Steel Magnolias in the Hour of Chaos Theory* capture chaos in the palm of the hand, and then release meaning back into the world about the importance of our roots and history. This collection is a powerful journey into the search for bloodlines and meaning. The poet finds ways to speak to the crucial stories that tell us about our origins and how they can define us and redefine us throughout a lifetime. The details and metaphor are woven in an artful way. Anyone reading these poems will carry layers of elegies and explorations with them, long after closing the book.

In stepping into this collection, one will find the alchemy of loss, and how the evolving stories of one family make for an exploration of mothers, fathers, stories, aunts, uncles, loneliness and a reconciliation of sorrow. In turning the pages, one will stand facing the ocean, discover how to grow orchids, how to be polite to birds, contemplate last rites, and a burial at sea. There is much to behold in this masterful book and one will be compelled to examine "the endless equations calibrated on night's chalkboard."

Connie Post

Poet Laureate Emerita of Livermore, California, 2005–2009,
author of *Floodwater*, winner of the 2014 Lyrebird Award

"James Cagney's writing is the type where if you do not savor each word, you will miss something vital and beautiful. Each piece is a story-world with its own rules, but somehow (impossibly) connects to the overall project. Please read any and everything James Cagney writes. You will be better for it."

Shawn Taylor

author, *Big Black Penis: Misadventures in Race and Masculinity*

"Here is the flora and fauna of a man searching and learning to understand family: blood, nurture, and the conjunctive experience that will bring him in relation. In these poems, I hear Cagney asking, where do I belong and who do I belong to? But most tenderly, held between Cagney's satirical storytelling, passionate syntax, and exacting images, is the poet being undone and done again by love. Love in its varying degrees of presence and absence. *Black Steel Magnolias in the Hour of Chaos Theory* is a beautiful book, insofar as Cagney is using poetry as the ritualistic intermediary to transform (familial, personal, and cultural) shame into beauty, into something that is useful for the living."

Arisa White

poet, author of *You're The Most Beautiful Thing That Happened*, *Hurrah's Nest*, and *Black Pearl*

NOMADIC PRESS

OAKLAND
111 FAIRMONT AVENUE
OAKLAND, CA 94611

BROOKLYN
475 KENT AVENUE #302
BROOKLYN, NY 11249

WWW.NOMADICPRESS.ORG

MASTHEAD
FOUNDING PUBLISHER
J. K. FOWLER

ASSOCIATE EDITOR
MICHAELA MULLIN

SECOND EDITION DESIGN
JEVOHN TYLER NEWSOME

MISSION STATEMENT

Through publications, events, and active community participation, Nomadic Press collectively weaves together platforms for intentionally marginalized voices to take their rightful place within the world of the written and spoken word. Through our limited means, we are simply attempting to help right the centuries' old violence and silencing that should never have occurred in the first place and build alliances and community partnerships with others who share a collective vision for a future far better than today.

INVITATIONS

Nomadic Press wholeheartedly accepts invitations to read your work during our open reading period every year. To learn more or to extend an invitation, please visit: www.nomadicpress.org/invitations

DISTRIBUTION

Orders by teachers, libraries, trade bookstores, or wholesalers:

Nomadic Press Distribution
orders@nomadicpress.org

Small Press Distribution
spd@spdbooks.org
(510) 524-1668 / (800) 869-7553

Black Steel Magnolias in the Hour of Chaos Theory

This book was made possible by a loving community of chosen family and friends, old and new.

For author questions or to book a reading at your bookstore, university/school, or alternative establishment, please send an email to info@nomadicpress.org.

Back cover art: "Actual/Reflection" by Kathranne Knight

Published by Nomadic Press, 111 Fairmount Avenue, Oakland, California 94611

First printing, 2021

Library of Congress Cataloging-in-Publication Data

Title: ***Black Steel Magnolias in the Hour of Chaos Theory***
p. cm.
Summary: The poems in *Black Steel Magnolias In The Hour of Chaos Theory* interrogate identity, family, loneliness, and the expectations of masculinity. Using dreams, blues and a chorus of voices, this collection of poems examines the complexities of intimacy for an adopted person trying to find balance between two families—one rattled by age and illness; the other, holding space for a son that doesn't exist.

[1. Poetry. 2. Adoption. 3. Family. 4. Black Studies. 5. American General.] I. III. Title.

LIBRARY OF CONGRESS CONTROL NUMBER: 2021945156

ISBN: 978-1-955239-07-3

BLACK STEEL MAGNOLIAS IN THE HOUR OF CHAOS THEORY

JAMES CAGNEY

BLACK STEEL MAGNOLIAS IN THE HOUR OF CHAOS THEORY

JAMES CAGNEY

NOMADIC
PRESS

This book is dedicated to James and Juanita Cagney and Stephanie Chappel Williams and Stephen S. Green.

contents

foreword

I first met James Cagney in the '90s on the spoken word/poetry scene at La Peña Cultural Center in Berkeley. His literary genius stood out from the beginning, but it was also clear that there were stories he wasn't telling. As he cared for his dying mother, he told us all that poetry was his therapy. As I got to know him after his mother had passed away, it became clear that his family was a Winchester Mystery House of twists and turns. He would perform dazzling poems of political and religious metaphor and outrage, but never quite revealed much about his inner workings. I was even in a writing group where he began a haunting literary novel that he didn't seem to know how to end.

Decades later, I still recall some of the lines. At one point, James joined a writing workshop of mine called The Brotherhood of Truth Telling at La Peña. I started it to support the men in that writing community in becoming more authentic in their work. In the early 2000s, we went to Cave Canem together and it was there that he began the slow process of unravelling some of himself to weave into his narratives. Our lives have diverged in the last decade since I became a mom who doesn't go out much at night. However, I was fortunate enough to attend the launch of his poetry book, *Black Steel Magnolias in the Hour of Chaos Theory*. As the book's description suggests, "the poems...interrogate identity, family, loneliness, and the expectations of masculinity...examin[ing] the complexities of intimacy for an adopted person trying to find balance between two families—one rattled by age and illness; the other, holding space for a son that doesn't exist."

I have always loved James' work, but it is a joy to bear witness to this collection, to see the fulfillment of his literary promise, and to finally hear the stories that young genius was unable to find words for so many years ago.

Aya de León
author of the award-winning *Justice Hustlers* series,
Equality Girls and the Purple Reflecto-ray
and *A Spy in the Struggle*

introduction

Poems are neither sworn nor obligated to tell the truth, but in my practice emotional honesty is important. I am drawn to courageous poetry. With the opportunity to publish my first book, it felt important that I use those pages to introduce myself with my heart presented first.

This collection of poems works as autobiography. I never intended this, however over the years a book's worth of poems on family and memory accumulated. Poems that made sense together and told a story. I spent many hours on the floor of my bedroom and at tables in the public library beginning to form questions I had no idea how or who to ask. Writing helped unthread the mental knot I clumsily tied attempting to figure things out alone. Poems are perfect little machines for unanswerable questions.

When I was born, my mother gave me to her teacher at the beauty school where she studied. Reasons, if you want them, were money and a rough series of years with my biological father, whom I never met—and who died years before I was informed I was adopted. My birth mother intended to reclaim me after 4 or 5 years but didn't. As a child, I met my sister once, without ever learning her name nor who she was to me.

I credit the father who raised me for becoming a poet. I write poems to fill the silence that once existed between us. That hour and fifteen minutes mentioned in "Someone Else's Child" was the most important silence I ever encountered and contributed to, a silence I never wanted to experience again. There arose urgent conversations I needed to have, but had no safe place to turn, except the page. And who would listen or empathize, except those congregating at open mics in the Bay Area? I

learned as much listening to local poets as I did reading strangers Rita Dove, Gary Soto and Lucille Clifton. My heroes wrote and spoke their truths and didn't flinch. I wanted to tell my father I loved him without flinching and couldn't.

My life is not tragic. This isn't a story of abuse. The questions raised here are philosophical ones regarding identity and family and adoption. As an adult adoptee, where should my loyalties be directed? When I met my biological family, no one ever asked about my childhood. To them, my memories and family of origin were irrelevant. After my parents' death, did the extended family I grew up with view me as a kind of subcontractor, now liberated to do as I please? What happens to the memories I had of the family who raised me? What happens to their stories considering I was the only one who knew and remembered them?

The long title, *Black Steel Magnolias In The Hour Of Chaos Theory*, is a poem itself. It's a private joke understood intuitively. It is a collage of words caged in a draft email I could neither finish nor send. I stand as a combination of two families, two stories, two names shuffled together. The title is me.

Since this book was first published, a few friends confessed they had to put these poems down and walk away for a while. I took those words for a compliment. I have often wished I could put down my own life and walk away for a while but didn't, channelling that same energy into writing poems. Tap out whenever you want, but know that I am still working out the combination, still shuffling identities. There is no proper introduction for this book. How do you introduce an infant to the new life laid out before them except to say, Go and see!

James Cagney
June 20, 2021

THE BIOLOGY OF RANDOM INTENTION

I frowned over the soft zodiac of brown wrinkles
attempting to squint clarity

into my palm's cracked plate
as if it might be a map to someplace

important. I, too, wanted to disappear
into others but was disappointingly singular.

Brandishing an encyclopedia,
I was stunned to learn along our personal

milky way that there were names for every pleat
& channel, every mount of flesh.

Fate line. Sun line. Money line.
Heart line. Head line. Life line.

My life line looked past repair.
A coaxial cable snipped, frayed.

Since my quilted palm was my mother's responsibility,
I asked her what these alien letters meant.

Every origami starts with a valley or mountain fold,
she said. Yours is the mountain. Yours is a life of work.

Your hand, she said, takes the shape
of the last thing spirit reaches for in its last darkness.

1.

Identity To Burn

You have to write a poem about identity, she says.
Well, when is you gon' write
about me? When is you gon' write about
your favorite sister?
I know I've given you enough material by now.

Look, she says. You got enough
identity for the whole class—
there may not be enough time
for anybody else to speak.
Identity, she says. This gon' be
the easiest poem you ever wrote.

Let's see—
Tell 'em how your family tree
wasn't what you thought it was
Tell 'em about how you was an only child
and at 19 found out you was adopted
and suddenly had this whole new identity
Tell 'em about how your momma had seven kids
to raise on one check
so she gave you to another family
so you'd have a better chance at life

Now, they was really too old to have kids
but you don't have to say that
you can say how your momma befriended your—

how you say it? Birth-momma?
while she was in beauty school—
Miss Cagney was her instructor, huh?
Yeah, Tell em that
Tell 'em you didn't know about us—your real family
You just thought you was all alone in this world
after your daddy died / your momma died
Tell 'em about how Medi-Cal did you a number
and you became homeless
and your other family said "Drop us a postcard
ev'ry now and then, Baby James
Let us know how you doin' / Let us know you alright."

Tell 'em bout how you was born, when? In '68?
and reborn in 1999
Adopted back into the family you was adopted out of

Now—you don't have to Tell 'em bout your love life
I'm saving up to get you a good piece for your birthday
and don't Tell 'em bout your brother that's been
institutionalized
or your cousin
with the plate in his head
who drank himself to death
after your momma passed.

Shoot! Can I get credit for this poem, too?
I mean look at you. So much has happened.
You got two whole identities
Two families. Two mommas.

One of 'em's gon' now, but you know
I mean, boy—you rolling
you got identity to burn
you can knock this poem out in a few minutes
throw some rhymes in there, it'll be all good

Then you can start writing
about something important
You can start writing about me
'cause I can't see how you made it
all these years
without me
and I can't imagine
why you're having problems
writing about identity

Bad Luck John

Momma laid me 'cross a log, let the river carry me down
Momma laid me 'cross a felled log, let the river carry me down
I'm going back to that river where my momma let me drown

Daddy's seed, hot as brandy, I was sprouted on a bed of shame
Daddy's secret burned like brandy, I was made in quiet shame
Momma hated what waited in her belly, the Lord never knew my name

Swaddled in Bible leaves, the deacon told me to pray
Deacon Murray fed me Bible leaves, told me I got to pray
Holy water caught fire and his church melted away

I'm Bad Luck John. Devil, kneel on one knee
Call me Bad Luck John. Devil, get down on one knee
God won't spit my name. Satan, pray to me

Incubators of the Damned

was there ever a child here
conceived
by loneliness and booze
when love was lost to us
brewed in the awful solitary
of a motel womb
growing like a weed on the white tongue
of an alcoholic's promise

was there ever a child here

for these hand-me-downs
of neuroses
who understood
our need for whiskey
for madness
who understood our
need for a god to cuss
and pray to in equal measure

was there ever a child here

in the seam between recipe and memory
collaged from the spare parts of
whipped ancestors
hitchhiking on texas highways with open
wound sunsets riding shotgun
strolling hungry along river banks moaning

their philosophy of flies
masturbating in the unique silence of a loveless house

but this child … but this child

when does life begin
to whom does life belong
when does a mother have the right to say
                                                                                no

whose child is this
who claims this child

was there ever a child here

to take care of us
as we awoke saluting
death from our throats
praying to true blackness
in colored ribbons
of mucus long as choir robes
stranded on warmed schoolyard benches
where even kids ridiculed for being poor
                                        dare not approach
printed on cartons recalled
for undrinkable milk
squirming & kicking in an unclaimed
crib [no number]
placed here
alone
as if by miracle

Mr. King

Mr. King lived across the street from us.
In his retirement, he would work the yard
of his corner house spending the day elbow
deep in grass and leaves, clipping his shrubs
into perfect geometric bulbs.

There has never been a lawn so evenly measured.

To Mr. King, I was a ridiculously fat child.
He would wince as I'd lumber towards him on my way
to the butcher or the bread outlet, then shake his head
mouthing the words *waste or shame*
where others might say hello.

Often, while he stood with my father talking over
things old men talk about—military shipyards,
Oklahoma in the '50s, ghosts in the scrapbook of the mind—
and I'd bear the misfortune to pass his house
on errand for my mother, he would point to me,
a shiny plump ham hock, and preach:

> *In the Navy, they'd sweat all that fat off ya'.*
> *Back in the service, my body was cut like a drill bit.*
> *Ought to get you up at 5:30 every morning,*
> *make you run these blocks a few times . . .*

I could imagine Mr. King unable to eat
at night for envisioning butter plastering

my cheeks, my lips frosted in dried ice cream scum,
or me finally exploding in chocolate
leaving potato-chip shrapnel on my bedroom wall.

Mr. King is dead now. His shrubs sloppy
and lawn nappy with weeds. His drill bit abs
have long since flaked to dust. What evidence
is there of him ever having lived except for me
whom he left here flowering so perfect and green?

Bakersfield

Aunt Pearl's grass appears painted,
each blade perfect and ripe for bleeding
should you pinch it between your fingernails.
Her dog, named Rat by a granddaughter
for obvious reasons, darts a stray mark
of ink across the lawn. He stops at his water
dish, boiling with sand, and chokes
down the liquid. From a distance,
he appears to be a curly black wig,
his tongue a perfect orange slice.

The heat is a curse in Bakersfield,
worrisome and mischievous as a mad
fly, even coaxing my mother into
shorts. It is a heat that hugs you,
sticks and burns. It is a heat that
settles over you like ash and is cured
only by watermelon and lemon popsicles.

Night comes slowly as if the sky
were being peeled in long strips
of blue banana skin. One at a time
the stars remove their shirts
revealing their random white bodies:
tiny stones littering a beach of black
sand. In the cooling darkness,
the sidewalks surrender tortured
memories of heat, and mimic hot coals.

Uncle Jerry sits on the cement porch.
The sky above him ripens to a deep
plum color as he unscrews a story
from a bottle and moths dance
their suicidal dance for the flickering
porch light which, at this moment,
is brighter and hotter than the sun.

Negro-Geist!

I. Daddy

old crow & jack daniels understood
my father, mouthfuls at a time.
jim bean & old forester
were uncles in hard glass suits
they'd roll up in the knuckle
crack & sigh of hennessy
taking its first breath, then hound
dog laughter & dominoes
falling in hail on the grave
yard of the dining room table.

relatives who existed
only through stories & memory
would ease in like zombies on ropes of
blue marlboro & newport & camel smoke
then demand a séance in spades, coon can
& texas hold em
no wonder they call it spirits!

spirits baited my father with
courvoisier, snatching him out of his body
like a river catfish & he'd vanish—like that!
spirits made him burn-rubber-scream
in the driveway, stand on my bed, a sloppy
marionette & speak in tongues
or just toss pans & skillets at midnight.

I wouldn't see his ass again
till the next afternoon, looking
like something had chewed
all the sugar out of him & spit
the gray pulp on the couch.

II. Johnny

my cousin johnny volunteered
for possession every week.
spirits lit that nigga up like vesuvius.
he was certified!
electroshock exorcisms did nothing
empty bottles & cans
were his weekend storm warning—
old english, colt 45, crazy horse,
cisco—they'd demand sacrifices
in blood so bottles of
haldol & thorazine
would dice roll under the couch

friday nights, then doors
slam to splinters, tables
get flipped, walls
kicked until strait
jackets lay waiting on
the lawn.
momma would cite visions
of gang boys with tire-iron erections

& johnny's convertible skull
with its metal vent as if
it explained anything.
it didn't.
tween dusk friday & dawn saturday
he'd still be ready to
blow this muthafucka up.

You want some of this?

Do. You. Want. Some of this?

oh no oh yes oh no oh yes
I'll be damned I'll be damned I'll be damned!

Compare Your Childhood To How Your Father Handled Catfish

I. Night digging with shovels of light / the aroused orgy of earthworms churn in the black-cake flesh beneath my father's benediction of beer / a holy transformative act offered these creatures / busy stretch- crawling through our fingers like drunks rolling home

II. Tolerate the brisk flies munching your ears at the river / the dervish ecstasies of their black seed bodies stumbling through the air / their hot electric praise song psalm for the spiked jewelry of the river / holy ghost dancing in my father's palm like a fresh-bathed infant and shining like Reno money

III. Toss the river's perfumed bounty into an igloo cooler / a crib for purgatories eggless black sperm to run infinite loops until dizzy and confused / The mad gasping of the largest one— smooth as a boxer's bicep / paraded through a witness of neighborhood drunks as if prom king / How they all tearfully confess their preference for Old Crow over blessed water / how every living thing is saved until baited by sin and tossed into the tanks of hell

IV. Hold down the leathery armored samurai / delirious with color / swatting away sunlight / with its church-fantail / Peel the skin down like stockings for the buttery musculature beneath / its cologne close to rain / Click open the coin purse of its belly / boil a bath of baby oil while dusting the baby in a vestment of spices / Align a plate with the wet gold leaves of their palm hot bodies / Open your mouth as if to offer grace / but say nothing

I Learned Crazy From My Cousin John Edward

terrify your mother until her hands weep.
use your aunt as a substitute —she'll help you

get new apartments every year, be your sole visitor
in art deco hospitals that serve hypodermic lunches.

know the police by name. know god by name.
know the devil by name—but get them confused.

sleep in the park when the walls
start closing in. be polite to birds.

sprinkle lithium on your breakfast cereal.
draw perfect freehand apostles and arch

angels drifting down like puppets from orange
and yellow heavens. misquote parts of revelation

that best articulate your case.
sit at bus stops and stare wide-eyed

at the hot bowl of the sun. burst
apartment walls open with your heart.

keep secrets that would blow up the earth
but let no one forget you have that power.

talk shit to demons and pick your afro
with the rib cages of angels.

get drunk and become angry moses.
use furniture for tablets. warn the voices

partying within about the nature of god's wrath.
use malt liquor for holy water.

crucify yourself.

know everyone

awaiting your second coming   is dead.

Blood Strangers

I.

I never told you about the summer I kept
a regular correspondence with my mother (my
mother, yet not my mother) after she moved to
Louisiana. This was a year or more after we'd
first met. I was 20. In one letter, I wrote her
about a dream. In it, my sister Avis (my blood
sister) mailed me an envelope I opened over
a coffee table and photographs swam out like fish.
This dream was triggered after seeing a young man
on the bus one night—Avis' male twin, down
to the freckles scattered across his nose.
I wondered if we were related. I wanted to say
something or stare at him and could do neither.
It was dark with rain like angry bird wings
and I pretended to watch the water fanning beneath
the moving bus but instead looked at his reflection,
looked at my sister, looked at me. It was
then I realized there exists a contingent of people
in the world who all look alike and belong
together. This is called family, but I didn't know
that. In my family, I favored no one and
for us that was normal. I wrote my mother
(who was my mother, yet not my mother) about
this and in reply she mailed me an envelope
fat with un-narrated pictures of my blood strangers.
They were people I didn't know yet all variations
of me, as if they were practice sketches of
faces before the creator settled on mine.

II.

I never told you that my mother (who was
not my mother, yet was my mother) was custodian
of family photos. Rare cells of aunts and uncles in
their black + white lives. At my mother's funeral
the house popped with relatives who stuffed their purses
and pockets with photographs until, while waving in the
driveway, genealogical collages autumned from their coattails.
My aunt, promoted curator, harvested photographs from the lawn.
The family let go. My mother (not my mother)
and my father (not my father) claimed responsibility.
Without them, no one owed me anything.Not even love.

III.

I never told you about the time I grabbed
my brother (not my brother) after work one Friday.
That morning I rolled a blunt at breakfast, hid
it in the office, then asked him to join
me for a 4 o'clock potluck. He bought a bottle
of Hennessy from the liquor store across from
the hotel, then we sat at the pier exchanging the
sacred texts of our lives. We finished drinking, smoking
and stumbled back to his house. Once home, he
turned to his mother—young and healthy and not
my mother—and mentioned a story he told about his uncle.
She corrected him. That wasn't Uncle   . That was
Uncle   ! Back when we lived on   . And
they stood in the kitchen, exchanging names like playing
Speed. Then she picked up the Sacred Book, opened
it, and began turning pages, apologizing. I hope this
isn't too much, she said. You're probably sick of

hearing about people you don't know, she said. But
she couldn't stop. I didn't want her to stop.
They got church-loud, reenacting scenes. Some photos—they
hollered. Other faces would appear and the page quietly turned.

IV.

I never told you about my girlfriend (no
longer my girlfriend) and when I first met her
family. Her mother stared me down and called the
name of her own brother whom she said I
resembled. I did. I walked the corridor of her
house and saw him— his face a close runner-
up to mine. I stared at his photograph like
looking at my own, but in a dream, where
details are soft and malleable. He stood with his
half dozen siblings, folded like wings around seated elders.
This photograph was crowned with a gallery of my
girl (no longer my girl) and her family. All
in various stages of happy youth. Sometimes, in the
dim morning light of her room, I could almost
see the roll call of those photos in her sleeping
face. She has a family. I didn't know what I had.
A life that felt like someone else's. Through her
I've learned feelings are transient and impatient.
Even now: it seems she was holding me for someone
else, holding me to give me away.
In her arms, I was floating debris, unmoored,
and this is why she so easily sailed away.
Her place in the book is saved. What am I
but a story taken down annually off the shelf?
Do you remember the time? Can you recall his name?
Then, quietly turn the page.

Re: The Other Boy

i cried today because i was sad /
but also unhappy because i missed

so much / you do not always get a chance
to make up time / even so / God has been

good / i hope you are fine / did you get
another girl yet / try and try again /

she's out there / waitin' on her some james /
i dont know / i got five boys and four of

them is single / i think i will open
a marriage shop / you know when i was young

i used to write poems / so you are an apple /
wish i'd saved them / i tried to write

a book but i have trouble with my hands
and can hardly type anyways / there's too

much water under the bridge to keep track
of every drop / i would like to get

another letter from you sometime /
when you feel like it / do you ever see

that young lady any more or did that
one go on out yonder / i sometimes look

back on my life / ((NOT YOU)) / and wonder what
if i had married the other boy / what

would be diff'rent / you know i loved your dad
and treated him well in spite of the way

things were / but i loved the other boy too
and diff'rently / and one time after your

dad died we got together / we went to
a motel in his town / he was still with

his wife / its maybe hard for people to
believe but it was for no other

reason than to talk / we talked most of the
night / he told me how he left home when we

were teens and returned after i graduated
high school thinking i was still available /

but i was married to your dad then / he
said we cannot live in the same town now /

i am leaving here never to return /
and all them years his mom never told me

where he went but that's history / i would
not mess with his life now and we were too

old to have had an affair / that would've been
awful / so that night we just stayed in that

motel for hours / we could not figure
anything out / now you know a secret

about your mom no one else knows / isnt
that funny / will write again when i am

lonely / ok / i hope its ok / i love you, james
– R

The Fire In Her Eyes Redefines An Apple

The ritual of fruit begins again in June
when buckets of smiling plums and blistered peaches
arrive for her in cars, altering our kitchen into a
steaming workshop. Soon,
blackened pots boil with
life's winter blood. She quickly
buries the dead in a cemetery of
sugar, where apricots and pears await to be
baptized and born again as jam & jelly.

Late summer brings chopped
cabbages, cucumbers and ancient
spices, all bathed in a sauna of
hot vinegar and crushed red peppers.
The walls of our kitchen come alive
with the sweat of our ancestors
who live again through recipes.
The dead continue to feed the living with
greasy fingers, stuffing our mouths
with history's sweet cuisine.

Momma leads us to her garden and motions
over a field of greens, their vibrant
tongues lapping sunlight like thirsty dogs.
She tells us, "This is a lost art,"
and warns that our wives
will be useless to our children.

Weeping, she presents
the bouquet of her hands
fragrant with 40 years of
stewed tomatoes, summer squash,
sweet corns & candied yams.

She forecasts her death and instructs
us to sprinkle her body with salt
until her skin appears wild with dandelions—
place her in our biggest pot
and simmer to a low gravy.
Seal her in a glass-jar tomb.
Store her in a cool, dry place
and wait until the fog of poverty
settles in the valley of our ignorance,
when there's only rainwater,
credited bread, and the
memory of meat.

New Monia or Cognac For Water

Her voice tattered as a blues musician who drank cognac for water.
Weeks before tonight, before the prayers, before the flowers & dark
car even, I stood over momma watching her choke on the plastic air tube
the ER docs funneled into her throat. I stood above her, just us in the hallway,
my hands dumb and useless. What did she see in my eyes? Happiness.
I was *happy* this is helping, right? RIGHT? ... but that was then.
Now, in a corroded voice, she sits up in bed, tells everything
she overheard the graveyard nurses do during the late shift last night.
Boy, what you could get for five dollars and a medical supply closet:
Hermaphrodites! Horny orderlies! Hot love affairs! These freaks
love helping the sick. But they're sick too, momma says. Worse
than the drug addicts she used to teach at the beauty school... And
Right Then, momma's old friend Theresa walks into the hospital room.
She sits at her bedside, quietly takes out her eyes and polishes them
with the napkin she holds tight as a microphone wired to heaven.
Momma says (talking over Theresa's tears, speaking now of the man
who buried so many of our relatives): *Tell Thompson, get ready*
for another funeral. Theresa says: *Oh, Miss Cagney. Stop it.*
I say: Nothing. I look out at the sky, beaten purple-black from the storm.
Strobe lightning. God is too busy playing paparazzi for any prayers tonight.
I'd forgotten how momma had been so frightened of thunder.
God is talking, she used to say. Fill your mouth with prayers for forgiveness.
But compared to this new monia, to a body coughing itself empty,
to a husband's infidelity with death and his orgasm of earthworms,
to useless me, even ... This? This is nothing. Nothing, do you hear?
Theresa and her pity having long since gone ... Now, it's us, again.

And God, vogueing in the background. Now, momma says:
Where was I at? Oh, yes. Them hermaphrodite nurses. Them bad boys they got working here at night. Let me tell you what happened.
Oh God, how we laughed.

The Apartment

There are three of us here: my mother, her illness & me.
She fever-rolls beneath white fabric on the sofa.
I kneel on the floor next to her as she sleeps.
Her breath vindictive in her lungs. The apartment
door swings open and my best friend enters,
loud & toothy. He snaps x-ray photo-
graphs of me in helpless responsibility. A waterfall
of paper whitecaps the coffee table.
He laughs too hard to notice my tears. He says:
I'll call when I get downstairs.

I crawl towards the bathroom where
my oldest sister stands, arrogant & impatient, blocking
the doorway. She exhales a chest full of cigarette
smoke that hiccups a dirty thunderstorm along
the ceiling. I beg her to stop. She sneers: *The
pitifulness of yourself.*

The bathroom is mossy. The toilet black.
Towels in the sink, sentient & scarred. The phone
howls in the hallway, a lupine blues. What's
left of my sister dissipates in the smoke. Was
she ever there? My mother stands in the living room
her body an avalanche of silk & cotton.
She is possessed by a cancer the doctors do not believe in.
It curses through her & sings, sings, sings. The phone
harmonizes in G minor. The bathroom
where I stand, is a cage.

I Feel A Scream Coming On

Out of the blood-soaked silence
like a child buried in a ravine
whose spirit tugs at your sleeve
& hair like the wind

I feel it coming
over the horizon of the bitter truth
that nobody believes you're really sick
till you're dead
& pain is just a cry for attention

I feel it coming out of the clairvoyant silence
that haunts this house
like neon mice
& shivers deep in the shadows
where your ugliest secrets hide
& watch your uneasy sleep

I feel it simmering down in my gut
where compassion has fermented into hate
& has become a demon fetus
eating its way through vulnerable tissue & bone

It's coming out of my subconscious
whispering mantras I don't need
to be reminded of. I already know:
What's coursing through my veins
is deeper than the blues.

Even my boss can see I'm worried
after I hang up the phone. He asks
if everything is alright
& like a fool—
for the first time in my life
I tell the truth & say:
"No . . .
Everything is NOT alright & may never be."

She's the one sick.

But I'm the one who NEEDS to be taken care of.

While my boss rambles
I swallow shots of blood as I bite down
on my tongue. Meanwhile, he paces, preaches.
His words fall from his mouth in stones
& roll to my anxious feet. He says:
"Things Change. This Too Shall Pass.
Nothing Stays Fixed Forever."
He says: "Maybe you ought to pray.
I don't believe in God," he says. "But I believe
in being quiet. I believe in Love
& Peace."

Meanwhile, I'm thinking:

FUCK this existential theological
psychobabble masturbatory sixties
hippie yuppie motivational infomercial

self help BULLSHIT

Peace is what you get when you ask for pie
or ass— & even then you only get what you pay for

I don't need quotes from the bible or an advice column—
I need a bar fight.
I need a cheap, ugly whore with an accent
& a bottle of something that tastes like
swallowing a snake on fire.
I need to be arrested, irresponsible & mad.
I need a lead pipe & a jaw

I NEED
to sink my claws into a mutha-fuckaz chest
deep as a black head & sharpen
my teeth on his gizzard

I feel a scream coming on

I'm looking for somebody to mug me.
To say: *Gimme all ya got!*
So at first I can pretend to rifle
through my pockets
for bones or lozenges of blood
then I can grab him by his neck
look him in the eye & say:
You just brought a pistol
to a nuclear war, son!
That sound you hear growling like a thundering train
is coming out of my throat.

It is bile with tentacles.
It is a sound that eats
& right now
it is all I got
to give

Someone Else's Child

I'm going to write a poem about you, I said.
Should I tell the truth or just make something up?
What you'd write about me?
I'd write about the small things. Like catching
my first perch on a cane pole and accidentally slapping you
upside the head with it. It was the last time I fished,
you know that? You cussed the waters black. Mad.
I never touched a fishing pole again.
Why would you want to write that?
Silence. Do you remember when Mom
tried teaching me to ride a bike?
No. Let me hear it.

Why I Can't Ride a Bike

I outweigh my
mother by at least 50 lbs. though
her effort to help find my balance
is more colossal than any man's. My
father, fingers rooted in pockets,
watches us from a distance
like we're on a channel
he'd like to turn.

That's a sad poem, he said. Can't
you write nothing happy?
Not with you in it.
But I ain't never hit you. Thumped
your head once or twice.

Mostly I'm stuck remembering what we never did.
Share something. Play catch, even.
Wasn't no athlete. Tried
teaching you how to drive.
Sitting next to me on the freeway
holding the steering wheel doesn't count.
Well—ain't had nobody teach me
none of them things either.
Did you ever hold me when I was a baby?
Naw. 'fraid I'd drop you. 'sides. You were someone
else's child. Didn't think we'd keep you very long.
Thought for a while she'd come take you back to your people.

…If you wrote a poem about right now. About us
here in this room, how would it go?

Last Rites

While sitting with my father,
waiting for his end, white tubes
sprouting in wintry branches,
I watch the hospital clock.
See us men—watching one another
not look at each other
for one hour and fifteen minutes.
Somehow in that ridiculous gulf
of time it never occurred to
either of us to even say
I love you.

All you write, he said, are sad poems.
What would you have me write?
The truth. Your poem ought to be called
Fuk It. With no 'c'.
And it should go like this:

He did
the best he
could with
what he had
and he ain't
had nothing
'cept the blues

The End.

Empty of Apologies

I think maybe I'd like to apologize, but who to?
Robert Blake as "Perry" in *In Cold Blood*
(1967, Dir. Richard Brooks)

When we met, my mother's first words were:
        I know you hate me.

She apologized for all the element
that aligned prior to my birth

Told me she was: Sorry
                I'd been born
her body rejecting me like a plastic organ

I loved your father, but

...Sometimes, when I'm alone

apologies hiccup out of me
like sesame seeds launched off the lip

non-directionally

as if my brain were an encyclopedia
        stuttering with errors

Sorry   — I couldn't do more.

— I couldn't Be more.
— I couldn't bail cancer from my father's body as water
from a sinking vessel

My adoptive mother was *Sorry*
For her secrets *Sorry*
She couldn't be my real mother *Sorry*

My namesake couldn't get an erection
for anything in our house
except booze

...The second time I met my mother
it was like a blind date that wasn't going to work out

She said she was ____________

Don't look at my other children, she said,
closing her pocket-book. Look at me!
You slipped through my fingers unnoticed
like a seed that grew anyway.

I can't be your mother.
I can only be ____________

I took her hand, and despite it resembling my own
recognized how everything in her life ran onward without me

My mother made life by accident and was ____________

You think life belongs to you
until it's wrestled from your helpless arms

What last word will flick off your tongue then?

. . . My father couldn't make a life
stick under his own roof

All he could make was other people's tears.

On his last morning, my father
looked past me into a sun
I couldn't be, I mean—*see.*
didn't cry.

What might you have said?

____

My father's last words were:
Poor Jun... Poor Jun...
Him having no time to explain anything

Him forgetting I *never* used the word: Junior
And for that
I Am Sorry

He yanked cords out of his ventilators

as if pulling weeds

His fists springing wild
with white lures,   eyes belligerent / certain

angry at Any Thing keeping him alive

My father was:

Sorry   for Nothing.

My adoptive mother, though...
On the day she died
it rained so hard
the asphalt loosened and boiled

At her bedside, I was   Sorry
I hadn't worked hard enough. I couldn't
stop what was coming.

She stared a thousand yards
past anywhere I could see,
then was snatched like a fish
through the hospital skylight

The morning rain and
stammering of her doctor's phone voice
fries like static on a station
that won't come in: ___________

Requiem

shut down the highway
there's nothing up ahead.
the catfish have stopped biting.
the great man is dead.

board up the liquor stores
hide the guns under the bed.
ol' river has run dry.
the great man is dead.

jump out the back window
your shirt quickly shed.
hit the ground running.
the great man is dead.

gamble your last check
the chil'ren don't need bread.
the cupboard will remain bare this year.
the great man is dead.

a fight breaks in the bar
broken glass and hot lead.
fire one off for Cowboy.
the great man is dead.

momma dances alone
an old 45 plays in her head.
love is now rationed.
the great man is dead.

this trail leads nowhere
in whose footsteps shall we tread?
fill up that hole, boy.
the great man is dead.

Open Letter to Henry

It is so strange,
the photograph
I was given of you,
because the man in it
is me
and not me.

It is me
in costume
it is me at a distance
squinted into focus.

Everything
I do not know
about myself
has been buried
with you.

As I
settle
into a man
I do not know
I've become
a mystery
to myself.

How many times
have I laughed

coughed
whispered
heard
your voice
echoing through me.

How many times
have I missed you
waving back at me
from behind
every mirror
while I
shaved
washed my hands
cut my hair.

How many times
have you touched me
with my own hand.

My inheritance
probably lies
in habits
that annoy me the most.

The sound
I make
clearing my throat
the broad toss
of my chest
when I walk

or the desolate
silence
we shared in our heads
in our empty rooms
in our isolated youth.

How many times
have we been
so alone
we overlooked
one another
standing
as close
as any man
can
to his own
shadow.

II.

Tomorrow's Sorrow

Tomorrow is not promised, momma used to say.
I think of momma and now of Linda
who yesterday ran out of tomorrows forever.

Linda, office sugar-bully, compulsive over-sharer
pollinating our hallways & break-rooms with stories and memories.
Linda, who never met a conjunction or run-on paragraph
she didn't like —
her story ends in the financial district
standing on a street-corner, mid-thought

the phone squeezed in her sweating palm like a handle
with nothing left *here* to hold onto

and how she just clicked off, witnesses said
as if some switch was flipped by an unseen, indifferent hand.
How Death lands at your feet like a bird with a lotto ball in its beak.

I promise to let you go / just one little thing / this'll be real short

You might find yourself, like Linda,

your body shivering cancer on a busy street corner
then Jump Cut To: a cold, waffle-thin mattress
and a device sweetly named Life Support
filling your mouth with plastic instead of candy.

There's no way not to be but slightly embarrassed by this
            and yet anxious! To force feed someone—*anyone*—
your story
...stuck shotgun on the bus, idling behind you at the grocery store.

I gotta tell ya / you think THAT'S something / reminds me of this one time

For all the stories falling from her like old receipts
                        no one would believe this

the one story she didn't share was when
weeks earlier — while still in the office at her desk, mind you,
she went hollow and immobile
and spent the night in emergency with her queer office-husband
left sitting bedside, knitting patience with his eyebrows

            Knit one hour / purl two hours

while she bled out a child's load of questions in every direction
him unable to even stoneskip a word across her flowing river of stories

Listen to this / Let me tell YOU / This was years ago

When she woke up on the operating table
spitting out anesthesia like sugarfree gum
rat-a-tat-tatting like Barney Rubble's Betty

What story   was she   reminded of   waking up
beneath the surgeon's steady timpani
of fingertips and scalpels – himself mid-story to an

annoyed audience in the O.R. –

Doc, you should see the look on your face / u know who u remind me of??

I told you this would be short.
I swear this won't be long.

Anyway . . .

Do you have time for a 'Self-Portrait in BBQ Ribs'?
Here it go:

The list of flavors and smells I miss from home could fill a cemetery.
I had no holiday guests beyond my own memory and pornographic greed

. . . and loneliness. Yes, loneliness.

It's July 4th, Saturday at the farmer's market rotisserie truck.
I buy a whole slab of ribs for $30.
The boy giftwraps this zipper of bone as carefully as you'd swaddle a baby. I shove the 2 x 4 of meat into my teardrop-shaped bag, then run to catch the bus home.
The loud cologne of meat rising on the bus like an erection
and I sit next to this woman
who couldn't be bothered with
ANYTHING,
so busy she was staring into her phone,
when she jumped

as if a car backfired,
and wiped her seat for grease.

When what had happened was— she caught whiff of my bag
leaking rich BBQ spices and
sauce like a loose hem on a ghost's wedding dress
but I said nothing and just smiled and rang for my stop and

I've gotten off the point / I'll let you go, but / You know what—this reminds me

Sickness never makes a good story. Neither does loneliness.

Loneliness. Childlessness. Read: Purposelessness.
A hollow smile well practiced
to the point of affliction.
It's a story I know too well.
It's why I would walk away anytime Linda'd approach and start in
on her old job /old friend /old story
that may or may not have even been true.
She thought I hated her for her stories
stories she would have told anyway, in a vacant room or hallway
ricocheting her voice, her mouth busy as bird wings.

Waitaminnit: Did I ever finish telling you about the ribs?

Real quick: Do you feel more pity for the animal
that gave its life for my weekend lust
or for the Me standing at the stove, alone,
gently peeling back foil panties.
Me dowsing intimacy with this Braille of bone,

its scent hooking my brain's easy distraction,
my mouth again confusing prayer with begging,
when really it was searching the contours of air for gratitude.

OK—Not to cut this off / I promise I won't hold you / looklooklook

I don't know what it is to die
but I know the quiet deaths that kill us daily.
For example, something in me quietly passed away
while looking into my mother's face —
            she was strapped to a gurney in emergency, a hose
shoved into
her throat big as a water bottle.
                        Right then was no time for my stage-
fright. It didn't occur to me then
to tell a joke or a story. Though, years later,
it occurred to me to scoop up Linda and her loveseat-
body into my arms—mid-sentence—and hold her
while her stories wept over my shoulders.

Shed your memories like bird feathers, I'd whisper.
My heart, your dream-catcher.

Tell me how you've heard this one before.
Tell me how hugging can be a form of assault. Tell this story,
especially if you don't believe in God - the invisible
wire strummed between people like
everything that cannot be told, or every unspoken
apology. Tell my mother:

Momma, I had a joke that would have killed you.

But I'm sorry for my dumb bedside manner.
Tell Linda, I'm sorry for my back and a slowly-closing door
that her voice mistook for hatred, like a birdwatcher
mistaking a purple finch for a house finch.

But can't you see:

Mom, Linda—it was just me
trying to get a word in edgewise:

I don't have time for this / Maybe tomorrow

Road to Revival

for Dr. Maya Angelou

Illuminated triangle crowned by the sun

The call of this road soft as a mother's voice

Awaken to the living river of this road
Don't confuse poison for sugar on this road

Get lost just to be saved on this road
Dance for your testimony on this road

Be *On The Battlefield* on this road

Use this path to step into your greatness

Be casually brave on this road
Stay fierce in your faith on this road
Tell the truth till *Glory Hallelujah* on this road

Step into your courage
Bolster your spirit

Know Your Divinity

On the tongue that lifts faith above chaos
On the hands that built cradles when caskets were requested
On the pyramids, on the pyres, on the pulse of this new day

Know Your Divinity

In the sanctuaries
In the sickrooms
In the gardens

In the office of politics
On the borders, in the matrix

Know Your Divinity

In the bordellos with backroom nurseries
In the family reunions behind every prison wall

Know your elegance
Know your voice
Know your heart is not meant for storage

Know if they call for rifles someone must still bring bread

Know that last night something was said
And right at that moment, a man   a woman   was healed

Between the president and the mendicant
Between silk and steel conjoined above the fire
Between the tongue's knife and the lover's caress

Burns the Blues (of every hue)

The call to freedom on this road
The feathery touch of love on this road

The rituals on this road
The forgiveness on this road

Praise the Spirituals hanging like fruit above this road
                    that fill our mouths
                              yet remain whole & sweet for eternity

my dr says

my dr says   tell me everything
my dr says write down a list of all your meds
and I'll give you the exact date of your death

my dr says eating apples will thin your blood
my dr says vicodin makes pork tastes carbonated

my dr says a dozen crushed viagra
sprinkled over cappuccino
saved his marriage   and it wasn't worth saving

my dr has a portable liposuction machine
my dr says chicken fat
cures hypertension

my dr says
chew gum to fight depression

my dr says smoking weed is good for your prostate

my dr's license plate reads: ERECT DF

my dr says erectile dysfunction is caused
by insecurity   and there is no pill for that

my dr says avoid vegetables at all costs
my dr says *red meat red meat red meat*

my dr says finish this prescription tonight
and call him in the morning   if I can

my dr says
the primary complication of most surgeries
is the physician's hand falling asleep

my dr says if your meds
            have expired
                        crush them
                                    and put them
                                                into a pipe

my dr says the hole in the
                        ozone layer
is the creation of companies
that make suntan lotion
my dr says suntan lotion causes cancer
my dr says beach sand causes cancer
my dr says sometimes cancer just floats in the air

my dr says paxil   my dr says ritalin   my dr says salt

my dr says they use salt to preserve bodies
they salted Lenin, he's been dead more'n 100 years
            and looks better than half my living patients

my dr says eat more salt
eat salt until your teeth feel plastic

eat flour by the handful

my dr says: Bring Back Thalidomide

my dr says one of his patients
was on crystal meth—
            how he got that prescription, my dr. didn't know
my dr says the kid tried to commit suicide
by shooting
12 nails into his skull
with a nail gun

and he survived

my dr used a sterilized claw hammer
and charged him per nail

my dr says
those nails hold the degrees hanging in his office

my dr writes prescriptions in stick figures
                        on stained restaurant receipts

my dr says take four tablets with red wine
                                        and hold on

my dr says if I were you
I'd be dead by now
and they'd quarantine
my grave

Little Green House

having picked little green houses
from the compost pile all morning
she stares at her palms, sneering

fingers stretched into ninja stars.
It is now hours later but she remains
disgusted, as if her sparkling fingers

still drip in black sludge—a livid halo
of gnats around her. she stops herself
mid-story—everything freezes—

the pigeons, the car, the highway,
& she bounces back to her morning
spent plucking house berries

in the backyard, pronouncing this my
fault—me, the new roommate in the dog
house. That I didn't know the garbage

can was not for garbage—so what? I'm still guilty
by commission & therefore can not
be trusted. After dropping into the compost

bin a calendar page of monopoly houses
tangled in dust what will I NOT do?
But—this is not the end of it.

Her husband: "Now, honey—finish your
story about the birds . . ." And she says, "Yes!
In Montana, the pigeons think

they're hot shit!"
In her story, a whole flock
stood on the highway

like arrogant strikers daring her family's
approaching car as if birds had rights.
Can't you see them?

Bird chests heaving attitude
then fist-sized bodies ping-ponging
beneath the grill of a Ford,

the sound like monster hail,
feathers in violent orbit coughed
out from beneath the wheels,

car exhaust drizzling blood,
feathers and feces. But—
this is still not as bad

as the little green houses
that had to be plucked by hand—
no other way—from the tilting soft cliffs

of blackened banana peels and fruit cores,
so sweet & hot & delicious to the flies
dancing carbonated in air around her

cheering over that
which we were too full to eat.
Disgusting, she says.

Simply disgusting.

I Am Adopted

I am carrier of all stories and owner of none

At my birth there were no storks
Just an armada of perch and sunfish
guiding me naked/unmoored
down river on driftwood

The name of that river
flush with butter fat,
free-range babies
astride floating trunks
like a colony of frogs
was never said

Just this:

the tale of how I came to be in your family
without love's drunken regret
or teenage impropriety
but rather … a fishing trip
where the big one was me
as huge a surprise
as a tsunami

Imagine Plato aglitter in Vegas
or touring the chitlin circuit as a stand-up

This is how my truth was revealed
couched in a drunken comic's aside

I am the conjured one
& my life's story is his big closer

Think its easy making this shit up?
            Try inventing a real life

You are reflection of every previous face & posture
You are reflection of every memory recalled
            every shot of generational juice exchanged

I am the dust on your mirror
I am the crumpled receipt in your purse

I am adopted
(from the Latin word, meaning:
To pencil in; to opt for)

I am carrier of the virus of story

Along the fault lines cracking my heart
are inherited memories like viral jingles
for products they no longer make

You are my cousin / my brother / my niece
Yet I apologize that every time I see you
I must renew my vows

I hold the stories
your ancestors are too busy with death to explain

(If you can) put your phone away (long enough)
I can recite their ungooglable stories

Stories you'll soon learn the hard way:

I knew your grandparents & I ushered their funerals
I collected empty bourbon bottles during their Bid Whist games
I can remember them planting the fruit trees
          crowning your yard

I can remember your Aunt Effie saying:
                    You can hollow out the people
                    but they still carry the seed

Blood knows the melody
& ancient songs will play
through the pinch rollers of your
children's bones and habits

I am keeper of stories falling under the table
I am carrier of the virus of memory

I am adopted –
                    Too often my dreams are full of strangers
                    & my pockets full of someone else's keys

My burden is to know everything
and be asked nothing

          I was born   anyway
a kind of bastard with a license

I will have to be penciled in at the corners

my mug shot will have to be footnoted
in your family albums

I will be recalled like a ghost
haunting the smallest real estate
of your unused rooms

I will be fed everything you can't stomach

My mask is made to resemble your father
who taught me how to build a house
of bottles and fish bones
                                        but not how
to keep it warm
                              if I'm the only one in it

Bandon Beach

We race a drowsy sunset & storm
barrel rolling over the ocean
to return after 10 years to Bandon Beach.
Rain pin-wheeling before our car's headlights
like sparklers. We park beneath crawling sand
dunes sprouting seagrass & let the
motor idle. We stand near the cliff,
wind racing up from the beach 2 stories
beneath us at 60–70 mph,
turn our backs on the firing squad
of the ocean (this is ill-advised)
& lean into the soft coffin
of howling wind.

I turn to you, your eyes
fevered with happiness, & watch
you slide down the staircase
to a shoreline boiling milk white.
Basalt rock rising from the surf
in natural totems, bellowing to the
blackening sky like Shakespeare's
witches. Everything around us is alive
& wails. You run into the black
portal of a nearby cave & scream.

Here, in the chaos & shrapnel
of falling night, a scream is appropriate
shorthand for prayer. I run in after,

alighting the cold torch of my cell
phone. You rinse the peppery
sand from your palms beneath the pool
of alabaster light, confessing then how
you'd fallen while skipping down beach stairs,
rendered soft as flour. The cave, its scalloped,
reptilian walls, the soft palate of its floor,
is dependable & safe.
While outside, the sea roars its death song
& waves chew the shoreline.

We dare one another to leave first
while the tide soldiers forward
& night falls hard-drunk against the ocean.
All while the sea clamors towards us
harvesting screams from both our mouths,
leaving us, as one leaves a lover, speechless
& swallowed by darkness.

Holy Strata of Sweat & Skin

Pull up a blanket of topsoil
on the bank of this murmuring lakebed
and let the desert sing to us in the language
of sweet creosote and wild lavender

Thick gelatin of night carbonated with hot stars
reminds us how dependent we are
            on the milk of god's silence

Phosphorescent thighs of the moon
                                    cross and re-cross

Despite the debt of morning
making love here is the right thing to do

                        to subdue and splatter with whips of breath

The alternating current of pulses
beneath the bough of fingertips

Compared to myth and map of the tongue
beauty in the dark is useless

Stars watch us (with envy, as much as we do them)
            then faint   enchanted
out of the silent choir of the night sky

The galaxy above us, a sugar sonnet rhyming in planets,
                    while Asteria's fingers drip astrological omens

Silver oyster toenails
                    zipping gravel
                              mirrored beneath the braille sky

The sinking, the slipping, the listening
The smoothing, the sluicing, the lightning

The shifting dunes of an oceanic body
          (its orchestra conducted by a tongue)

So many routes for time's touch to take

          Column of bone, cross of rubber

The smiling white ship of the bareback moon
          Stars from its cratered eyes
                    shoot like dice across night's velvet floor

Vigil For Vespers (Opus No. 38)

If each star were a flame fountaining
beneath an onyx teepee
then let elder tongues
in an orbit of whispering moth wings
lick the flames with stories.

The milky way is here because I am here
and it is well worth crying over.
I cannot stop offering my own
solar system of ghost-pepper tears.

The endless equations calibrated on night's chalkboard,
a tarot of planets scattered across the topographical
map of the sky's arachnid body.

Bet the coins between corpses teeth that all the hoaxes
of love dissolve to moon dust back home.

I am less a crumb on the lip of this lake,
how its tongue sleepwalks a language
night often mistranslates in dreams.

The harmonic choir of cutthroat trout
sounds cribbed from the pages of Rachmaninoff's
lost rhapsody—a tragedy in silence

lulling me into this all-night vigil for vespers
and starlight's uneasy correspondence with gravity.

It's hard to lie quietly in the unmade bed of a prehistoric crater
with its sweet sheets of sagebrush
and not consider love's offices bankrupt and ridiculed back home.

Burial at Sea: Memorial Lighthouse, Trinidad Civil Club, Trinidad, Ca.

Bone spur of the lighthouse
excavated from the hillside
by diligent shovels of weather
stands purified under the administration
of the sun—overseer to an ocean
of scales flashing white and green.

An old man sits at a bench
shepherding the wet painting of the horizon.

As we approach, he pulls the loaded rifle
of his terrier closer to his chest.

They await what has already arrived—
the radiant ignition of ocean,
the coastlines dancers of granite and basalt
tossing gowns of sheer water,
foam livid in their teeth.

My friend and I stand on a cliff between
a small lighthouse and a brick wall. We stink
of endless afternoons of gravel and coffee—
yet the dog stays at peace in the old man's lap.

Over the hymn of ocean,
my friend, compelled by spirit,
turns to me, announces:
I want to be reborn
as a lighthouse.

I imagine him conducting
an orchestra of waves,
his tongue an aero beacon
slicing fog like cake.

We turn to the
stone wall behind us and read
the engraved names of those
lost and buried at sea.

The ocean, both city and cemetery—
the taken and the disappeared
remain as letters to a vacated name
and the range of years they were responsible for.

Were they buried with illness' intent?
Or lost to the endless curiosity of the waves.

What circumstances in life
will lead you to step into the mystery
of what fevers beneath the surface of the sea?

Will you be weather or rock or lighthouse
or letters assembled in combination
to unlock a tomb?

Perhaps the afterlife isn't above
but below. Perhaps dog and man
know this and wait

for the opening of the sacred text,
for seagulls to chant names
into the rock wall canvas,
for lyrics of the ocean's song to be revealed.

Like children, we approach the old man
inquiring as to the appetite
and habits of the lighthouse
and its ocean.

But the old man only turns
to stare through us and silently
mourn our sanity, as black fleas
drip from his dog's chest
like blood clots.

Lycanthropoetry

I.

The sky is pierced with a white nipple
lactating spirits. The pulsing moon drips starry
night sweats through the hourglass
of celestial consciousness. The moon,
growing a beard of clouds, demands sacrifice
from its sterile, onyx altar. It is a full, virginal apple
having never known the homicidal
climax of the teeth or the tongue.

This glacier of foam summons
the ache of a storm to pelt this feverish earth
with fangtooth rain, buzzing the air
in a squadron of hornets.

Houses, graves for the living, inhale steam
through the bronchial lungs of loose windows,
whose sudden sneeze in the night can startle ghosts.

II.

The striptease of night begins
with a dark purple strap falling through the blushed gloaming,
freckled with alabaster goose bumps. The moon hangs
above our campsite, a glowing white spider with a its
thorax full of silk, sitting lotus in a netting of stars—
each polished to a perfect, happy silver.

On our backs, we study the sky,
watching it shift in color, an undulating ocean of chameleons.
We pick the stars bobbing along the surface of night
and stuff our pockets with them
as a child might stuff her mouth with cake.

Climbing the ribs of our tent,
patient, curious and silent as a thought,
the moon leaves a shiny trail of neon
as it crawls the earth on delicate insect legs.

Know that the sound of light
raking cool sand is like that
of a panicked beetle
skittering across your casket.

III.

Private Boxes

Confusing confession with prayer again
what to let go versus what to take in
here—in this place, one of ten unconventional
places to confess, so says this dog-eared article.

Thinking   and not thinking   of my father
buoyant, drunk and drifting away on ivory sheets
thru the moon's shadow oceans.

                If money were no object,
what would I pay for an ounce of his
attention and forgiveness now?

I kneel—this altar a crossroads of teeth
at his mouth's unused apologies.

        Showing myself approved or worthy
of something resembling love, but not. This
holy burlesque   this sacrament.

            Blessed water
runs a freight train of blood through
the weary hollers of my cheeks.

I awake from yesterday's coma fluent in shame.
I open my mouth like an orphaned nestling.

            This is called supplication.

What catches in my throat—unnamable
until i looks up to I
            which is another way of saying
begging for acceptance is a fool's' errand
                        endarkening us all.

Anyone watching couldn't imagine I was praying
to be filled with a harvest of tenderness,
the most common seasoning of touch. How they'd critique
my nest — an inverted mushroom of fronds
left blooming champagne butter in the dark.

II.

New psalms are being composed for instruments
we never knew existed. Duets zippering like
perfect puzzle pieces we never thought to
put together. The fermented melody
is in the key of honey. Let us play.

III.

                        Did you know Genesis
birds learned to sing by accident?
By excitedly punching air from one another mid-flight?
The soft choke of their harmony like
mini church bells calling One
            to fall into attention and come home.

IV.

You had one job and couldn't do it since
grace is a corny prayer in your generation's mouth

Dizzied by what arrives embedded in every dawn
change is a blend of whiskey yawning in the mouth

Triumphant color and call all comes together now
in the diaphanous blossom of your radiant mouth

My name is an untreated fungus left
to dream bloom in your dark winter's mouth

I paid for this posture with hummed lullabies
the currency exchange for the static canticle in your mouth

Scoop buttery marrow sweating through bone
till new skeleton weeds grow wild in your garden's mouth

With the inflamed urgency of the ocean I climb
your body's ladder of scars with my narcotic mouth

Touch, Abstraction

There are hospitals where hands are a type of medicine
I smooth the tremulous lines along your temples with my palm
In these cellular rooms, bodies are worshipped in religions of disrepair
We burden our mouths to carry more than language

I align your tremulous temples in the rooms of my palm
There are hospitals where medicine is better than hands
In our mouths, bodies become religions and are worshipped with tongues
We trust our language to carry more than we understand

I align your cellular temples with hospitals and hands, hospitals and hands
That burden our medicines with lines of disrepair
We praise the smooth bodies in our mouths with psalms of worship
We trust our tremulous language more than religions

My palms carry sparkling medicines into your temple
Our bodies don't understand worship or religions
We cannot trust our language any more than our mouths
Some temples are better than hospitals and some medicines useless

Every. Body. I. Worship. Suffers.
Tremulous religions carried in the hands of language

The Sound Between Two People

I'm ghost-riding a picnic table,
orbiting empty cafes & drowsy trees.
The tables are freckled with calcified
black beans & the broken chips of yellow leaves.

Its 8:30 Monday morning.
I'm here to peacefully study before class,
when just above me begins the flurry
of a young woman's voice.

Her sound showers down from
the ring of open apartment windows.
Sharp inhalations as if she eagerly drowns
in all of what thaws & melts within.

The sound belongs to the morning
                & comforts me,
its spark jumping the distance between us—
                until I look up
at the courtyard entrance
                & see a shadow—a stranger
I just met the other day.

She steps into the sunlight
baring her own luminescence—
flowing drapery of braids & fabric.
She sits next to me at the table.

I speak loudly over the aria she never hears.

What happens is this:

for the first time in over a year,
I find myself speaking meaningfully
about writing.

I plead into this stranger's hands
for community & understanding.

From where do you harvest?
How do you translate experience into
a praise song, a language of divinity
that might feed the world?

How might you even account
for the sounds that play us into existence?

She said: Being a writer
is like being a bad psychic.

This intimacy, between my heart
& her ear, these testimonials
of what nudges us
towards conversation between ourselves & God
                                        is the missing element
                                        in my girlfriend's kiss.

The tongue has unlimited fluency,
how it knows the flavor of even the fibers holding

our words together, yet so often
it never says what needs to be heard
between two people.

This woman
never hears the morning song
now mellowed into a cool drizzle,
never sees me blush, even as we touch hands
before branching off
to different classes & stories.

Yet she stays with me,

the secret bonding agent
for every unnamed thing
rattling loose
while I'm hallucinating a future
in my girlfriend's arms.

Caught Up in the Rapture

I remember when the world
was supposed to end.

It'd been scheduled hella times
& kept getting pushed back.

That last time was a Saturday.
Granted, the man forecasting it was old,

probably confusing the world's end
with his own. But he kept a bible open

on one knee and pounded the floor
with his walking gavel, sneezing Repent.

I didn't know what repenting was
so I spent the day drinking.

All afternoon I watched Dirty Junior
convert a V6 Mustang to dual exhausts.

He sawed steel pipes by hand while
the rest of us lazy bastards drank 211s in devotion,

ate preposterous sandwiches &
laughed at the manic doodles of

his sister's rat terrier. Somebody decided
we should all go out again later that night,

especially since Junior had to work all day.
So I came home to take a nap

but couldn't, because the news kept
promising that this was the end.

& the old oracle with the stick
held a press conference from his deathbed

& the newscasters all looked
pallid & nervous. I couldn't stand it.

I went outside to call my girlfriend
to tell her I was still stuck in the city.

Yeah, I was lying. Standing at the bus
stop for optimum background noise

so I didn't have to work hard to sell
my excuse. It was okay.

She was probably taking
communion from a bar stool.

We wished each other good night
& made future promises. Yeah,

we lied to one another. While I kept
my eyes on the suture of the horizon

expecting it to loosen & snap &
grandmothers to hover mid-air like gnats

or a kissed seed head. But no one floated
anywhere. Nothing caught fire.

No one, from where I stood, even
hollered. If not today, someday.

Nothing lasts forever.
I neglected to tell her that.

But by the time it occurred to me,
we'd already hung up.

Walk of Shame

That night I shallow-slept with fire
licking inside my eyelids   I dreamed an auto bio-documentary,
A *Mother's Mistake*, and re-imagined being born to a mother
who sneered
like a debutante returning her first plate to its kitchen.
I wept myself awake then & listened to my bedmate snore—
her sweet surge of breath rhyming with the
burgeoning streets below. I longed to know, to touch
the foreign machine of her,
          less than a pillow's thickness away.

But in our first kiss, her mouth clamped to a smirk
                    as if it held a shot of sour medicine;
          as if she could taste how I was mismanufactured
& bio-chemically rinsed in a steel sink to be filed under a stranger's
name & address.

She   slept   supernaturally   while all night,
I watched the dark-
ness as if it might disobey. I expected my father's phantom to
emerge like an alligator from the room's horizon of shadows—
          I believe in ghosts, because I am used to the intimacy
in cold spots
but nothing moved except the Morse code prayer of my pulse.

That next morning I stared at the undifferentiated
tissue of my body—a key unlocking nothing.
It didn't matter which word tickled, turning on her tongue,

or locked me in the solitary closet of my body.

This is mostly about the mind, isn't it?
    The expectations of failure;
the familiar spirit of personal cruelty.
    The deliquescent nature of
relationships & how I think of my father whenever women look past
me.
        Here's the real question I'd like to ask my father:

    What might you have told your real son about the nature of
love-
claiming it, feeding it, keeping it alive in spite of its instinct to thrive
                                        without
you?
What might you tell a son you loved
    about the hieroglyphics of bodies
        or the nature of culling desire—
    as a man, what exactly should I surrender to?

Let me answer the question you have of me: No.
You were my idol. Of course I don't know how to love
        but I know how to be shamed
& no two tears fall or taste the same.

The Night You Came Home From The Bar & Wept

The kitchen walls will never forgive this
splatter pattern of grease. These
past midnight notes from your throat
like a saxophone thrown from the roof
of a burning cathedral.

Who let the dogma of loneliness out?
Who frowns over strippers? Who uses tears for lube?
Who gets headaches from their own touch?

Don't mythologize a legacy of whisky-colored thighs,
knowing you kiss knuckles for the ground's embrace.
Save your algorithm of excuses.
            Your mirror is more dependable than God
            & just as silent.

You were leaving the bar after trivia night
& the ground was scarred from weeping, or was it
just you? You'll sleep hard enough to
dream away the shattered pancakes of glass puzzling the floor

—forget the failed recipe of porn on the kitchen computer
& how you held yourself & cussed
like you needed an exorcism.

A hole can only be defined by its edges.
I'm not talking about your heart.
Press your skin until it yields
chemical shame. Cover your wounds with lime.

The tinnitus in your ears? Sweet nothings.
Ignore them. They're hymns of lost spirits,
their skull-tongues fluent with dead songs.

Only Now Do I Understand How to Grow Orchids

For one optimistic spring, I
hosted a leonine orchid
only to have its season
of supernatural color
weep leaves on my
kitchen floor. How all my relationships end,
her dripping color
naked & frustrated in my hand.

Its baby-teeth leaves loosened
& huddled in a geometric puzzle
swept by obsessive-compulsive wind
leaking in thru the broken window.

For years I conceded failure in
the language of the beautiful,
confused by the dreamy delicacy
with which color & texture kiss the eye.

But you—Mistress of the Complicated—
every week your office down the hall
hosts a rotating color wheel of Friday mood orchids,

flowers I learned to pity simply due
to the hand that rears them.

Riding the elevator one morning
after working in the same office five years—
only then did I begin to understand
the mystery behind life that eludes even
the topsoil leaking through my fingers.

My name less than the foam
popping in your cheek.
Our daily gaze half-meeting
without a splinter of kindness to fall.
Your eyes not even daring to judge my shoes
(like the ashy mouths of starving children
interrupting your shows at night).

But You—Reedy & Milky & Easy
with God's good favor—
Your bouquet of gratitude
blackens to burned at your altar
from lack of food & light.

How at once I wondered
what you wouldn't dare reveal.

How even your preferential gaze
trims the variety of truth from this world.

Until the Friday morning I swung the office
kitchen door open & saw your
flustered Filipina secretary
wrestling with the octopus branches

of a selenipedium over the sink,
her fists dripping coconut husk chips like foreign coins.

She loves her flowers, the woman
turned to me & said.
If it was left to her,
they'd end up dead.

Eucharist of Shame In The Office Storage Closet

The cleric / the body / the cheering blood. The spoonfuls of honey
    I expect to heal me.
The price of acceptance is to kneel on faith in this velvet darkness.
Take – eat! He says, again, *again!* and once empty of incense,
    shyly closes,
        like a flower, or a fist.
From somewhere in the dark behind me rises a beeping noise.
I turn towards the rooms' electric pulse. There sits a hospital bed
amongst the boxes.

I approach, stand bedside.

I am a nurse holding a baby.
    The baby is me.

The woman on the bed is shaking her head
        No. Just no.

I am a motherless child before I've had a chance
to be mothered *or* a child.

I am dry-drowning. My mouth, a hot pond of anointed sea-foam.
The Morse Code of mechanical beeping tells me the figure on the bed is dying.

The figure on the bed: <u>a stranger.</u>
        No—*I* am the stranger.

The figure on the bed: <u>my birth mother.</u>
                                        No.

The figure on the bed is my adoptive father,
still drunk from Winter, 1968.

He appears devoured by a quicksand bed licking its sheets.

Behind me, Young Jehovah closes his docket.
Says: *I'm running late. I gotta get back. I gotta go... I gotta . . .*

We cool? (Door opens)

We cool? (Click)

What I cannot say, machines speak for me in a syncopated orchestra.
My birth mother snaps shut like a purse.
My father looks through me for a sun not risen.
He squints at me through a gauzy, medicinal haze
like gazing thru cigar smoke greasing the air of a bar.
                                                    Poor Jun, he says. Poor Jun.
His eyes blurred / watery / melting in his skull. *Poor Jun*, he repeats
like a rosary. *Poor Jun*, he says over and over
                                                            till it's over.

Before My Friend's Reception, I Stand Facing The Ocean

It is my second ocean this week—this one's waves gnashing its teeth in a grimace between laughing and chewing. The sky, burdened and exasperated by fog. I am that fog. And I attend this wedding detached as a ghost.   Beneath these waves churn the surface of my first ocean, bathwater-warm beneath a blushing sky. There the waves were littered with people like flotsam after a storm. The ocean would eat the naked alive. Just now, a dog runs the length of beach like a jet nearing take off, his hind legs flaring red in joy. Somewhere people spill from the mouth of a church beneath a steady hail of rice. Somewhere people laugh in the presence of roses and the foamy ejaculate of champagne. Somewhere in the space between that previous ocean and this, someone floats forgotten, and drowns. Blankets have been folded and sand is spanked off flat soles, while someone bobbles, their arms like antennas on a channel no God is surfing. Their mouths engorged with starfish, new tongues stuttering death's forbidden name. If I could, I'd swim out and save them myself — but the drowning swimmer is me. (No, this is not a dream) In the flipside ocean, I stand with green water belted at my waist, afraid to be swept off my feet. I scoop up the loose nuts and bolts of seashells rolling beneath my toes when waves are inhaled away from the beach and the water level bows. Here, I stand weeping fog and sea foam, humbling myself to learn from a dog. He snatches the steaming meat pumping in my chest and

runs for the mountains, a pile of discarded jackets, before looking back longingly to ask: Do you get it? Between these two oceans floats a bottle with blues lyrics, telling my life. The bottle floats along the embryonic ocean like a jewel slipped loose. You know, I was once thought to've been extinct, and scientists were disappointed to find me alive. I was discovered using an abacus of sand dollars, counting the inventory of waves. I'm going to lie down on this cold brown-sugar sand and await the dog's return lap. With my luck, I'll be found having drowned in nothing. There'll be traces of two oceans in my system, my eyes dripping saline rivulets
in different flavors. Ah, but first—the wedding...

reading guide

Artists, writers, and students of all levels are encouraged to use this section of Black Steel Magnolias In The Hour of Chaos Theory to inspire new work. These prompts come from the poems themselves and can be used for creative writing and poetry workshops.

Place and Memory

In which cities or towns or roads do your childhood memories take place?

- What became of the child you once were? Do they still thrive within or have they matured and moved on?
- Describe the house from your childhood.
- Describe nightfall from your childhood bedroom. What sounds would you hear?
- Describe a childhood road trip or vacation.

What are the primary elements found within your memories: water, earth or ______?

- Write a poem for a family member.

- Write a poem intended for the ocean.

- Describe a place or location as if it were a person.

Write a poem where a bed is made. What speaks as you begin to sleep?

- In which location do your dreams take place? Describe it by touch.

- Why can't we smell anything in our dreams?

Representative Poem(s):

"Bakersfield" (pp. 13)

"Negro-Geist" (pp. 15)

"Compare Yr Childhood To How Yr Father
Handled Catfish" (pp. 18)

"I Learned Crazy From My Cousin John Edward" (pp. 19)

"The Apartment" (pp. 31)

"Bandon Beach" (pp. 70)

"Holy Strata of Sweat and Skin" (pp. 72)

"Vigil for Vespers (Opus No. 38)" (pp. 74)

"Burial at Sea: Memorial Lighthouse
Trinidad Civic Club Trinidad Ca." (pp. 76)

"Before My Friend's Wedding Reception I Stand Facing
The Ocean" (pp. 104)

Conversing With The Past

Imagine a relative in your family from 100 years ago or more.

- What would you ask your ancestor? Write their response.
- What do you imagine your ancestor wants or would expect from you?
- Write a poem that celebrates something from the past.
- Interview your grandparent. Choose a story to convert into a poem.
- Write a poem to inspire future generations.
- Imagine your words can heal. Where do you send them? What do you say?

Representative Poem(s):

"The Fire In Her Eyes Redefines an Apple" (pp. 27)

"Someone Else's Child" (pp. 36)

"Requiem" (pp. 43)

"Open Letter to Henry" (pp. 45)

"Road to Revival" (pp. 57)

"I Am Adopted" (pp. 66)

Honoring One's Body (And Its Imperfections)

What are your best flaws? Which part of your body is most neglected?

- Write in praise of your dents and scratches.
- Write a love poem for something you don't do well.
- Write a love poem to your back, to your armpit, to your ears.
- Give your toes voices.
- Have your eyebrows ever met?
- Write a poem about a tattoo.
- Write to the Mother and Father within yourself.
- Write a poem about something rarely appreciated.
- Write to someone who has never seen you.
- Write a poem about how you want to be seen.

Representative Poem(s):

"Biology of Random Intention" (pp. 1)
"Mr. King" (pp. 11)
"Touch, Abstraction" (pp. 88)

Using Voice, Monologue and Dialogue in Poetry

- What's a story only you can tell?
- Consider how your friends and family tell their stories.
- Who tells the best stories? What is unique to how they communicate?
- Who speaks loudest in your house? Who speaks softest?
- Write a poem using a specific voice.
- What have you never said?
- What do you know for certain: tell two truths and one lie.

Representative Poem(s):

"Identity to Burn" (pp. 5)
"Tomorrow's Sorrow" (pp. 51)
"Little Green Houses" (pp. 63)

Knick-knacks and Artifacts

- As a child, which toys did you share with special friends? What song does that toy sing between uses?
- Use an old family photograph and write a new introduction to it. Mention something that cannot be seen in the photograph.
- What was the best gift you've ever given or received?
- Describe a person by what is in their pockets.
- Describe your ______ by items that they left behind or owned. What items do you remember as being important to someone else?

Representative Poem(s):

"Blood Strangers" (pp. 21)
"Re: The Other Boy" (pp. 24)
"Open Letter to Henry" (pp. 45)

Letting Go and Moving On

Pretend that your pen or keyboard is a kind of hammer: Write what needs to be destroyed.

- List your recurring thoughts. What do you still wish you could get over?

- What can or cannot be erased?

- Write what happens when you walk away.

Representative Poem(s):

"Private Boxes" (pp. 85)
"Walk of Shame" (pp. 95)
"Eucharist of Shame in the Office
Storage Closet" (pp. 102)

acknowledgments

This book exists because of the faith and encouragement of J. K. Fowler and the staff at Nomadic Press. Special thank you to Michaela Mullin for taking this journey one line at a time.

My eternal love and thanks to Joanna Spencer and Dorian Spencer for starting me on this journey. None of these poems would be worth reading without the Cave Canem family of poets and the foundational work of Toi Derricotte and Cornelius Eady.

Extra special thanks to My Holy Trinity In The Word: Opal Palmer Adisa, Aya De Leon, and devorah major. They nurtured and educated me in the ways of poetry, as did Richard Moore (a.k.a. Paradise) and his Afrometropolitan Poetry Series, and Jennifer Joseph and her Sunday nights at Poetry Above Paradise Lounge.

Pete Marshall has supported me and these poems since day one—more than I've ever truly been able to support him in return. Family has held space for me, yet I have never truly held space for family. Pete, turns out you were the man I should have tried to model myself after. How blind I am to what shines so close. This book is offered in grace, love, and gratitude to Pete and equally to Brandi Jonez, Joshua Marshall, and their families. Words here fail. Fool that I am, I dropped the ball and let it roll away.

Further special thanks and eternal gratitude are due to Dru Brown, Mahogany L. Browne, MK Chavez, Steve Cosgrove, Tongo Eisen-Martin, John Hayes, Jack Hirschman, David T. Hunt, Shane Koyczan, Naru Kwina, Psalm Lewis, Natasha Marin, Myron Michael, Tureeda Mikel, Ian C.D Moore, Khiry Malik Moore, Walter Mosley, The Family Nitoto (especially Sekou and Kele), Sharon Olds, Cyrene

Powell, Lisa Marie Rollins, sam sax, Stewart Shaw, Mike K. K. Smith, Terry Taplin, Shawn Taylor, Debbie Vinograd, Julia Vinograd, Ariana Waynes, and Arisa White.

Much love and thank you to Scott Hoag for the author photo, which Arthur Johnstone drew from.

I offer my deepest, sincerest gratitude to past and present editors of Susurrus journal in Sacramento for publishing many of the earliest poems in this collection. Thank you to Jan Haag and Heather Hutchinson for your support and encouragement of this work.

Respectful appreciation, honor, and loving acknowledgment to Dr. Maya Angelou, Angela Boyce, Linda Corbett, John Edward Johnson, Brian Lowe, Avis Marshall, and Rev. Robert Triplett.

I am humbled by, and thankful for, the lives, work, and memory of Reginald Lockett and Piri Thomas.

Without these people, there is no me, there is no poetry, there is no purpose. Thank you, all.

Thank you to the following publications, where some of these poems previously appeared:

Susurrus (2002): "Bakersfield"
Susurrus (2004): "I Feel A Scream Coming On," "The Fire In Her Eyes Redefines An Apple," and "Lycanthropoetry"
Susurrus (2006): "Mr. King"
Susurrus (2006) and Barbershop Chronicles (2008): "Someone Else's Child"
Ambush Review, Vol 2. (2011): "New Monia or Cognac For Water"
All The King's Horses: An Expression of Depression Vol. 3 (2011): "I Learned Crazy From My Cousin John Edward"

Fresh Hot Bread (June 2014): "The Apartment"
Print Oriented Bastards, Issue 8 (Fall 2015): "Compare Your Childhood to How Your Father Handled Catfish" (under a slightly different title online)
Eleven Eleven Journal, Issue 14 (November 2016): "Walk of Shame," "Before My Friends Wedding Reception, I Stand Facing The Ocean," "Little Green Houses"
Cosumnes River Journal (May 2017): "Bandon Beach"
Five80Split (Spring 2017): "Private Boxes" (awarded a poetry prize)

Some poems in this collection have also appeared in self-produced chapbooks between 1996 and 2016.

JAMES CAGNEY

James Cagney was born in Oakland, Ca., 1968. He was named after his father, a retired forklift mechanic. His mother, Juanita, worked as a beautician and teaching supervisor at several local beauty schools. Raised an only child, James was 19 before being told he was adopted. In his biological family, he was youngest of six. James' father was diagnosed with an asbestos related cancer the year he attempted to leave home for University. After his father's death, he supported his mother and grandfather until their deaths. In those intervening years, James studied writing and poetry independently, via the public library, workshops and the abundant open mic scene in the Bay Area.

James Cagney is a Cave Canem fellow. He has authored five self-produced chapbooks including "Dirty Thunderstorm," "Transmitting The Disease of Poetry," "Hot Death," "On The Road To Heaven in A Broken Down Truck," and "Greatest Hits." As a featured poet, James has performed in many venues, museums and programs throughout the San Francisco Bay Area, as well as Sacramento, Vancouver, Chicago, and Seattle. He appeared as a featured artist in Miko Kuro's Midnight Tea: Midnight in Mumbai (2012) and Celebration of The Word with Maya Angelou (2001). Visit his blog at thedirtyrat.blog.

cover missive

On "Actual/Reflection"

by the back-cover artist, Kathranne Knight

The drawing begins by laying my body on paper and tracing around it with pencil. It's an awkward and tender action to perform, this going around and around the body. I consider it a document of form and action, and the shape of its absence. The word, "actual" in the title alludes to how I made the drawing; that it is a head and hands traced there, "life-sized." The reflective tape makes room and implicates the viewer in the drawing. David Hammons' body prints, Ana Mendieta, and prehistoric handprints in the Cueva de los Manos are influences on the work.

color pencil and reflective tap on paper 14" x 11"

kathranneknight.com

NOMADIC PRESS
BLACK WRITERS FUND

NOMADIC PRESS
EMERGENCY FUND

OTHER WAYS TO SUPPORT NOMADIC PRESS' WRITERS

In 2020, two funds geared specifically toward supporting our writers were created: the **Nomadic Press Black Writers Fund** and the **Nomadic Press Emergency Fund.**

The former is a forever fund that puts money directly into the pockets of our Black writers. The latter provides up to $200 dignity-centered emergency grants to any of our writers in need.

Please consider supporting these funds. You can also more generally support Nomadic Press by donating to our general fund via nomadicpress.org/donate and by continuing to buy our books. As always, thank you for your support!

Scan here for more information and/or to donate.
You can also donate at nomadicpress.org/store.